LARGE PRINT

SUDOKU

Easy to Read Puzzles

SIRIUS

SIRIUS

This edition published in 2022 by Arcturus Publishing Limited
26/27 Bickels Yard, 151–153 Bermondsey Street,
London SE1 3HA

ISBN: 978-1-3988-2010-4
AD010680NT

Printed in China

Contents

An Introduction to Sudoku

Each puzzle begins with a grid in which some numbers are already placed:

	9	6			8		3	
		1		4	2			
5						8	1	9
4		7	1	2				3
		8	7		6	5		
2				9	4	6		1
8	7	2						5
			3	5		1		
	3		2			4	6	

You need to work out where the other numbers might fit. The numbers used in a sudoku puzzle are 1, 2, 3, 4, 5, 6, 7, 8 and 9 (0 is never used).

For example, in the top left box the number cannot be 9, 6, 8 or 3 (these numbers are already in the top row); nor 5, 4 or 2 (these numbers are already in the far left column); nor 1 (this number is already in the top left box of nine squares), so the number in the top left square is 7, since that is the only possible remaining number.

A completed puzzle is one where every row, every column and every box contains nine different numbers:

Column

Row →

Box →

7	9	6	5	1	8	2	3	4
3	8	1	9	4	2	7	5	6
5	2	4	6	7	3	8	1	9
4	6	7	1	2	5	9	8	3
9	1	8	7	3	6	5	4	2
2	5	3	8	9	4	6	7	1
8	7	2	4	6	1	3	9	5
6	4	9	3	5	7	1	2	8
1	3	5	2	8	9	4	6	7

3	4	5		9	2			6
			5				4	8
				4	6			2
	5	6	1		7	2	8	
1		3		2		7		4
	9	2	4		8	5	3	
2			6	7				
9	6				1			
5			2	8		6	1	3

5					1	9	7	2
	8	4	7			6		1
7			9	5			3	
8	9			1		7		
		3	6	8	5	2		
		2		7			1	5
	5			6	2			9
2		9			8	1	4	
3	1	8	4					6

	6			5	8			2
	5		1			8	9	6
4		3			6	7		
	7	9		6			5	1
		2	5	4	7	9		
8	4			1		6	2	
		8	4			1		3
1	2	4			3		7	
5			9	7			8	

5				8		4		3
	2	3	9		1		6	
		6	7		3		5	
1	4		6		7	3		9
	7			1			2	
2		8	3		5		1	4
	5		4		2	9		
	8		1		9	5	7	
9		2		7				6

				1	7	6		2
8		4			2	9		
		7	5		9			1
	6		8	9			7	
	3	8				1	6	
	9			6	1		4	
2			3		8	5		
		5	1			8		4
1		6	9	4				

4	1	9				6	8	7
7			4	9			2	3
	3	6	1			5		
3					5	7		
	7		6	3	8		4	
		1	2					9
		2			3	8	1	
6	4			2	1			5
1	8	7				4	3	2

7		1		5			4	6
			2	3	7			
5		8		1		9	7	
2	5	6	4					1
	4		7	9	2		8	
9					1	4	2	3
	7	2		4		1		9
			8	7	5			
4	6			2		8		7

8		3			7			2
	6		8		9		7	3
5				2	6	8	9	
	2		5			4		1
		7	9	4	3	5		
3		4			1		8	
	4	6	7	8				9
9	1		6		2		4	
7			1			2		5

			8		3			
8		5		4		7		1
3	1						8	6
		9	2		6	3		
1			4	5	7			9
		8	9		1	5		
7	4						5	2
2		3		7		6		8
			5		4			

5	8	6					9	2
	4	1		3		6		5
3		7		2	6			
	1				3	2		
8	3		4	6	9		1	7
		5	8				6	
			6	9		4		8
7		8		4		1	3	
9	2					7	5	6

	2	7	5			6	1	
6	9				1		7	4
	1			7			8	
			3	8		1		5
		9				4		
1		2		6	4			
	8			2			5	
3	6		7				2	8
	7	5			9	3	4	

			1	5	9			
	8	4						7
3	1			7		2		6
8	9	5	7			3		
	6		9		1		8	
		7			8	9	2	4
7		3		8			1	9
6						8	4	
			2	1	6			

★ ★

	3				2			5
	1	9			4	3	2	
		6	3	7	5	9		
7			2				3	
	4	8				7	6	
	5				6			1
		4	6	8	3	2		
	9	5	1			4	8	
6			4				7	

	6			8	3	5		
1	3		2					6
9					5	7	4	
6	8	1	4	9				
	7						2	
				5	1	8	6	9
	9	4	1					5
3					7		9	8
		2	3	4			7	

			5		2			6
			4	3	1			9
9	1	2		8				5
		4	8		6		9	
7	8						3	2
	9		2		3	6		
5				6		7	1	4
4			1	5	9			
8			7		4			

		4	8				1	
6			5			2	9	
5				1	9		4	3
	6			3		4		9
		3	9		5	8		
7		1		8			5	
4	7		1	2				6
	5	8			4			7
	2				7	9		

2	8			4		1	3	
6		4					9	
			7	2	9			
7	6	8			4	3		
4			8		2			9
		1	3			5	4	8
			2	5	8			
	3					6		4
	9	7		3			1	2

★ ★

	5	4			2	8	9	
1					5		4	
		8	4	7	1	6		
	4		5					7
	6	7				3	2	
9					6		1	
		5	6	3	4	2		
	7		2					6
	3	2	9			1	8	

★ ★

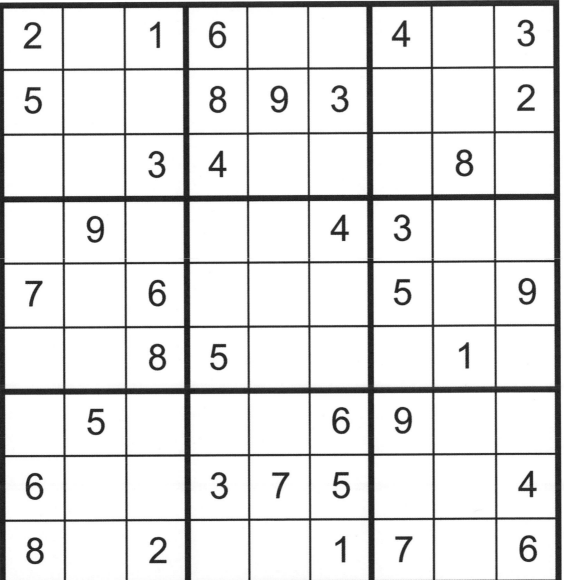

			6	1			5	
9			3				7	8
5	3	8				2		
		9		6	5	1	4	
	2		7		4		3	
	7	5	1	8		6		
		2				3	6	4
7	1				6			9
	5			2	9			

1		4			6	2		8
2					8		7	
		9	2	3	7	4		
	3		8					2
6		5				3		9
7					9		1	
		6	9	5	2	8		
	9		6					3
4		7	1			6		5

				1	7	4		2
1	6					7	8	
5				2		9	3	
		1			2		9	
4	9		3		6		2	8
	7		8			5		
	2	9		3				4
	5	4					1	6
8		3	7	6				

	2				9	7		8
					8		1	
7		1	3	5		6		
9		3	7			8		5
	4			3			6	
6		8			1	3		2
		5		6	2	4		7
	7		5					
1		9	4				5	

★ ★

		8	2		6			7
			8	7		4		5
9		3	5			2		
	2		7	4			3	
	1	9				7	4	
	4			2	9		8	
		6			7	9		3
7		4		3	2			
5			9		1	6		

		7		6	4			
1						3	7	2
	2	9			3		8	
6		5	7	4				8
		3	5		9	1		
4				2	6	9		7
	8		4			6	9	
3	5	4						1
			8	1		7		

		8	6		7		3	
	3				4	5	6	
	1	4		5	2			
1				2	6			9
7	6						4	1
2			4	1				5
			9	4		8	1	
	5	6	8				2	
	9		2		3	4		

★ ★

9	4		1			6		
	7	8		5	4	1		
	5		2					7
7		4		8			6	
2			4		1			8
	1			2		3		5
4					3		9	
		6	5	9		7	3	
		3			7		1	2

3	9		5	6		1		
	8						5		7
		4	2		1	6		
			9	5			7	1
	2		1		8		4	
6	1			3	2			
		8	7		9	4		
7		9						3
		6		4	3		9	2

7	4			5			3	6
		6	3		2	1		
	3			7			2	
3	8		7		9		1	5
		7	1		5	3		
1	2		4		3		9	7
	5			1			8	
		8	2		7	4		
4	7			9			6	1

	2	9	3	8			6	
4	6			7			3	8
					5	4		
3	8	1	4					9
5								7
9					1	8	2	4
		3	2					
6	9			5			8	1
	1			4	9	5	7	

★ ★ ★

	7						8	
2			6		5			9
3	1						2	5
		7	4	1	8	2		
		9	3	7	6	5		
5	3						4	8
4			2		9			1
	9						5	

	9						8	
	4		2		9		5	
3		7		6		2		1
1				7				8
			6		4			
8				9				5
5		3		4		9		2
	1		7		3		6	
	8						7	

★ ★ ★

9	1			5			3	2
	3		4		9		8	
	9	4				6	5	
6		1				7		8
	5	8				3	2	
	6		1		8		9	
4	8			2			7	5

3					2			9
	6	7						
	1	8		3				
			5			4		6
		3		1		8		
4		1			9			
				8		7	2	
						1	6	
5			6					8

★ ★ ★

	2		1		4		9	
				6				
1			9		2			7
2	3		4		8		5	6
		6		7		8		
9	8		6		5		7	2
3			8		9			5
				3				
	4		5		1		8	

1	8						6	7
		4				3		
7			1		3			4
	1			4			3	
8			5		1			2
	3			9			7	
5			3		2			6
		9				5		
2	4						8	3

		6	7	8			5	3
				2				
9	7						8	2
			9			5	4	
		5				9		
	9	3			4			
5	1						2	9
				9				
4	8			1	2	3		

	7		8		5		9	
8								6
		2	4		6	3		
7		6	5		2	8		1
9		5	1		3	4		7
		7	6		1	9		
4								3
	5		3		8		2	

		3		7				
1	4		9		6			
6	7		3		8			
	9		5		1		6	8
		6				5		
8	1		2		3		9	
			4		7		3	5
			6		2		8	7
				3		9		

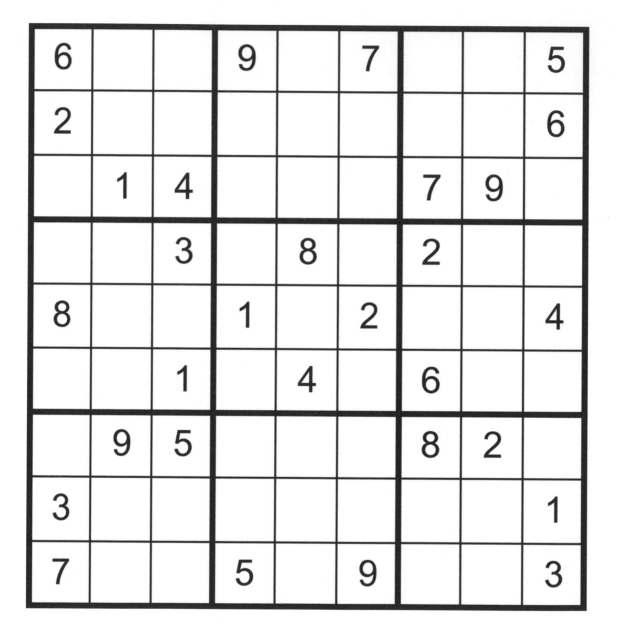

6			9		7			5
2								6
	1	4				7	9	
		3		8		2		
8			1		2			4
		1		4		6		
	9	5				8	2	
3								1
7			5		9			3

★ ★ ★

							4	
9		2	4	5		6		3
			3	9				
		4		6			9	
		6	7		9	1		
	1			8		4		
				3	8			
6		1		7	2	5		8
	7							

3	6						1	5
				3				
2	7			6	1	4		
			8			2	5	
		5				7		
	8	7			5			
		2	3	9			6	8
				5				
5	3						9	7

		9	3		8	6		
5								1
	8		4		1		7	
4			8	7	2			9
		7				2		
8			6	3	9			4
	4		2		3		1	
3								6
		5	9		7	3		

4			1		6			7
				8				
	6		5		7		1	
8	9		3		5		2	1
		3		4		8		
1	4		9		8		3	6
	3		7		9		5	
				2				
9			6		3			2

★ ★ ★

	3		2		6		7	
6				5				9
		1	7		3	8		
8		2				9		3
	1						2	
7		4				1		5
		6	8		2	3		
3				7				4
	7		9		5		1	

		6			2	9		
2	3							
8	5			6				
	4	2			9			
	6			3			1	
			7			4	3	
				1			6	3
							5	2
		7	8			1		

		2			7	8		
1	9			2	5			
3	7							
			8			3		
2				9				4
		7			6			
							7	9
			9	4			1	2
		6	5			4		

			4	3	9			
		5		2		9		
	6	3	8		5	4	2	
	5						4	
		8				1		
	9						3	
	4	6	1		8	7	5	
		1		4		8		
			6	7	2			

★ ★ ★

1			4		6			3
		5	2		7	8		
	9			8			1	
7	1						6	4
		4				5		
5	2						8	9
	7			2			3	
		8	3		4	1		
6			1		8			5

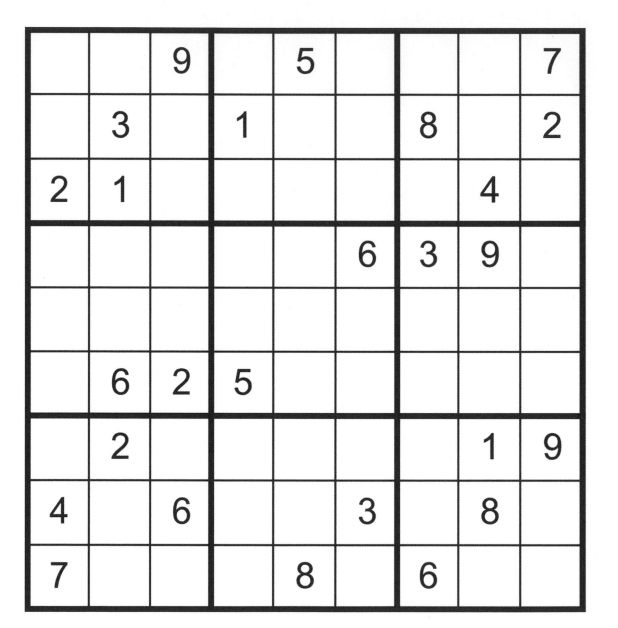

		9		5				7
	3		1			8		2
2	1						4	
					6	3	9	
	6	2	5					
	2						1	9
4		6			3		8	
7				8		6		

★ ★ ★

8			3		2			7
				4				
		3	7		8	5		
1		8	2		9	4		6
	4			5			9	
9		7	4		6	8		5
		1	9		7	6		
				1				
2			6		3			9

3				1		6	7	8
9					6			
8			2	3				
	2					1		
6	9						4	5
		8					2	
				4	8			2
			5					1
2	7	5		9				3

★ ★ ★

	4					8	5	
2		8			5		7	
		6		9				1
					9		3	8
7	1		3					
3				2		6		
	2		7				4	3
	5	1					8	

5						3		2
		4		7			1	
	1	6			9			7
					1		9	3
1	5		8					
9			2			5	7	
	3			8		4		
2		5						6

★ ★ ★

				5				
3	8						5	4
		2	3	4			7	6
8		7			9			
		6				8		
			8			6		9
4	9			1	5	7		
1	6						8	5
				8				

		4		7	8		6	2
8	9						3	7
				9				
					6	4		9
		9				3		
6		3	9					
				8				
2	8						9	1
3	4		1	2		5		

★ ★ ★

	8	9		7		3	1	
4			5		3			2
5								6
	1			9			6	
			4		7			
	6			5			2	
6								9
1			8		9			7
	2	8		4		5	3	

			9		3			
	6	3				5	8	
5		9				7		3
	3		5		1		6	
			8		2			
	1		7		4		9	
2		8				4		6
	9	4				3	7	
			2		6			

★ ★ ★

		5	8	3			9	6
				1				
1	8						3	7
	6	7			1			
		1				7		
			6			5	1	
8	9						2	1
				8				
5	7			9	2	4		

			8	1	3			
	3			9			4	
	8	9	7		4	6	1	
		1				3		
	5						7	
		8				4		
	2	4	5		7	8	6	
	7			8			5	
			6	2	9			

★ ★ ★ ★

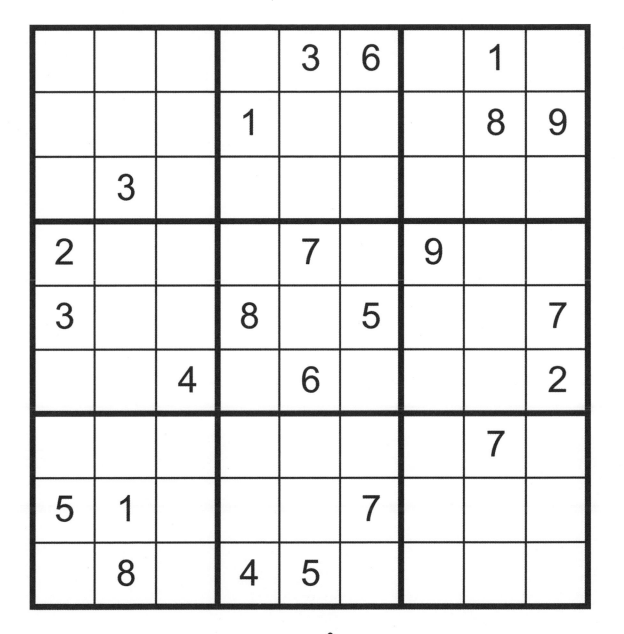

	4		9			8		
							5	7
		1	3			2		
		6	7				1	4
			1		8			
1	3				4	6		
		8			3	5		
3	5							
		4			5		7	

★ ★ ★ ★

	8							
			7					
			2	1			6	
7		2						1
5				3				8
6						9		4
	4			5	8			
					9			
							2	

					2	9		7
		7			8			
	8	4		6			2	
		1			9	3		8
5								2
8		2	6			7		
	1			9		6	4	
			3			8		
6		5	1					

★ ★ ★ ★

		8		6				
	7	6	2					
3		5						
7					5		1	9
	5		7		2		3	
6	1		8					4
						8		5
					4	7	9	
				9		1		

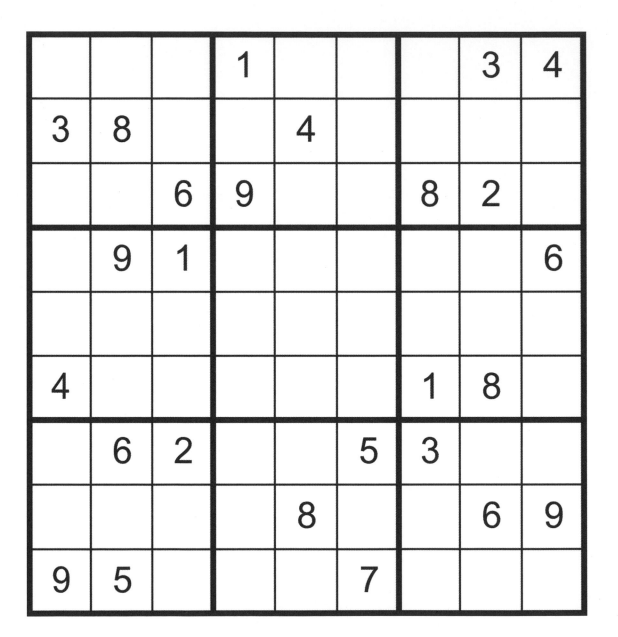

★ ★ ★ ★

			7	6			2	
					2			
		6					4	9
	6			1				8
1			8		6			3
5				4			9	
4	9					3		
			5					
	1			3	7			

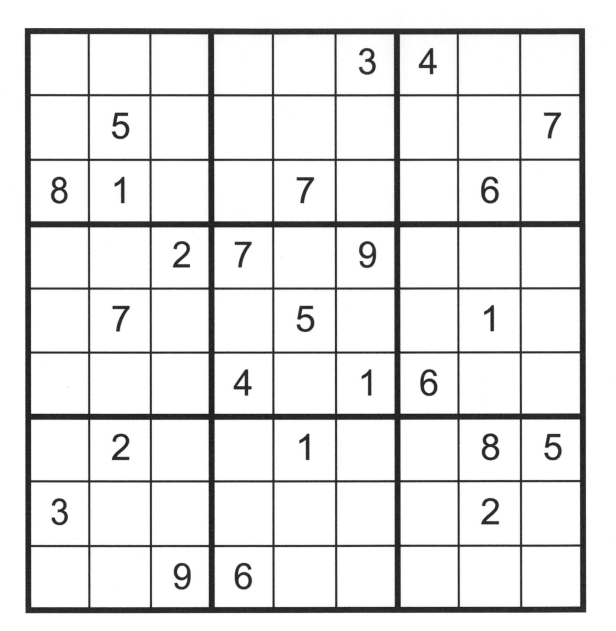

					3	4		
	5							7
8	1			7			6	
		2	7		9			
	7			5			1	
			4		1	6		
	2			1			8	5
3							2	
		9	6					

★ ★ ★ ★

8	3					4		
					7			
	1		5	4				
7				8			3	
1			9		6			4
	9			1				6
				9	5		2	
			2					
		9					8	3

8							2	5
		6		9				4
			1				7	
		9		6		2		
			7		1			
		3		5		1		
	6				7			
4				8		6		
2	5							9

★ ★ ★ ★

	6		2		9	1		3
		2				8		
	5			6	8			
			4				9	8
		4				5		
7	2				5			
			8	9			3	
		1				9		
8		5	7		3		4	

★ ★ ★ ★

	1	9			5			
	5		3	6				
							6	
		8		3				7
		4	2		1	6		
9				4		8		
	4							
				2	7		1	
			4			2	5	

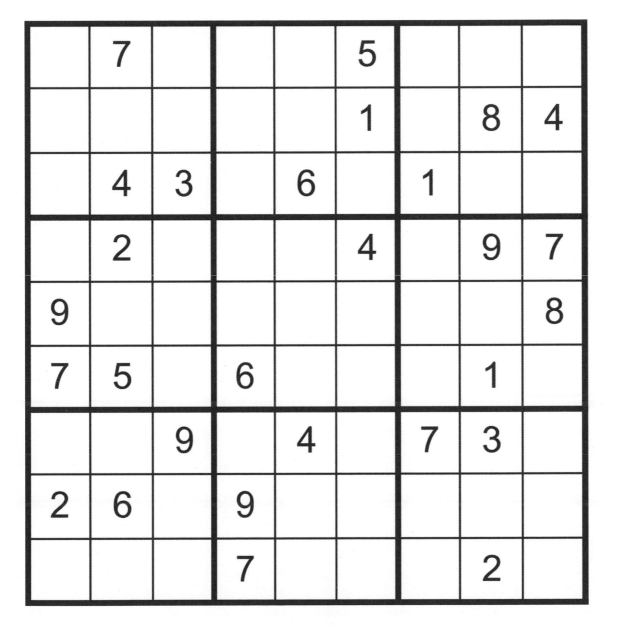

1

3	4	5	8	9	2	1	7	6
6	2	7	5	1	3	9	4	8
8	1	9	7	4	6	3	5	2
4	5	6	1	3	7	2	8	9
1	8	3	9	2	5	7	6	4
7	9	2	4	6	8	5	3	1
2	3	1	6	7	4	8	9	5
9	6	8	3	5	1	4	2	7
5	7	4	2	8	9	6	1	3

2

5	3	6	8	4	1	9	7	2
9	8	4	7	2	3	6	5	1
7	2	1	9	5	6	4	3	8
8	9	5	2	1	4	7	6	3
1	7	3	6	8	5	2	9	4
6	4	2	3	7	9	8	1	5
4	5	7	1	6	2	3	8	9
2	6	9	5	3	8	1	4	7
3	1	8	4	9	7	5	2	6

3

9	6	1	7	5	8	3	4	2
2	5	7	1	3	4	8	9	6
4	8	3	2	9	6	7	1	5
3	7	9	8	6	2	4	5	1
6	1	2	5	4	7	9	3	8
8	4	5	3	1	9	6	2	7
7	9	8	4	2	5	1	6	3
1	2	4	6	8	3	5	7	9
5	3	6	9	7	1	2	8	4

4

5	1	7	2	8	6	4	9	3
4	2	3	9	5	1	8	6	7
8	9	6	7	4	3	2	5	1
1	4	5	6	2	7	3	8	9
3	7	9	8	1	4	6	2	5
2	6	8	3	9	5	7	1	4
7	5	1	4	6	2	9	3	8
6	8	4	1	3	9	5	7	2
9	3	2	5	7	8	1	4	6

5

9	5	3	4	1	7	6	8	2
8	1	4	6	3	2	9	5	7
6	2	7	5	8	9	4	3	1
4	6	1	8	9	3	2	7	5
7	3	8	2	5	4	1	6	9
5	9	2	7	6	1	3	4	8
2	4	9	3	7	8	5	1	6
3	7	5	1	2	6	8	9	4
1	8	6	9	4	5	7	2	3

6

4	1	9	3	5	2	6	8	7
7	5	8	4	9	6	1	2	3
2	3	6	1	8	7	5	9	4
3	2	4	9	1	5	7	6	8
9	7	5	6	3	8	2	4	1
8	6	1	2	7	4	3	5	9
5	9	2	7	4	3	8	1	6
6	4	3	8	2	1	9	7	5
1	8	7	5	6	9	4	3	2

7

7	2	1	9	5	8	3	4	6
6	9	4	2	3	7	5	1	8
5	3	8	6	1	4	9	7	2
2	5	6	4	8	3	7	9	1
1	4	3	7	9	2	6	8	5
9	8	7	5	6	1	4	2	3
8	7	2	3	4	6	1	5	9
3	1	9	8	7	5	2	6	4
4	6	5	1	2	9	8	3	7

8

8	9	3	4	1	7	6	5	2
4	6	2	8	5	9	1	7	3
5	7	1	3	2	6	8	9	4
6	2	9	5	7	8	4	3	1
1	8	7	9	4	3	5	2	6
3	5	4	2	6	1	9	8	7
2	4	6	7	8	5	3	1	9
9	1	5	6	3	2	7	4	8
7	3	8	1	9	4	2	6	5

9

6	2	7	8	1	3	4	9	5
8	9	5	6	4	2	7	3	1
3	1	4	7	9	5	2	8	6
5	7	9	2	8	6	3	1	4
1	3	2	4	5	7	8	6	9
4	6	8	9	3	1	5	2	7
7	4	1	3	6	8	9	5	2
2	5	3	1	7	9	6	4	8
9	8	6	5	2	4	1	7	3

10

5	8	6	1	7	4	3	9	2
2	4	1	9	3	8	6	7	5
3	9	7	5	2	6	8	4	1
6	1	9	7	5	3	2	8	4
8	3	2	4	6	9	5	1	7
4	7	5	8	1	2	9	6	3
1	5	3	6	9	7	4	2	8
7	6	8	2	4	5	1	3	9
9	2	4	3	8	1	7	5	6

11

4	2	7	5	9	8	6	1	3
6	9	8	2	3	1	5	7	4
5	1	3	4	7	6	2	8	9
7	4	6	3	8	2	1	9	5
8	3	9	1	5	7	4	6	2
1	5	2	9	6	4	8	3	7
9	8	4	6	2	3	7	5	1
3	6	1	7	4	5	9	2	8
2	7	5	8	1	9	3	4	6

12

2	7	6	1	5	9	4	3	8
5	8	4	6	2	3	1	9	7
3	1	9	8	7	4	2	5	6
8	9	5	7	4	2	3	6	1
4	6	2	9	3	1	7	8	5
1	3	7	5	6	8	9	2	4
7	2	3	4	8	5	6	1	9
6	5	1	3	9	7	8	4	2
9	4	8	2	1	6	5	7	3

13

8	3	7	9	1	2	6	4	5
5	1	9	8	6	4	3	2	7
4	2	6	3	7	5	9	1	8
7	6	1	2	9	8	5	3	4
9	4	8	5	3	1	7	6	2
2	5	3	7	4	6	8	9	1
1	7	4	6	8	3	2	5	9
3	9	5	1	2	7	4	8	6
6	8	2	4	5	9	1	7	3

14

4	6	7	9	8	3	5	1	2
1	3	5	2	7	4	9	8	6
9	2	8	6	1	5	7	4	3
6	8	1	4	9	2	3	5	7
5	7	9	8	3	6	1	2	4
2	4	3	7	5	1	8	6	9
7	9	4	1	6	8	2	3	5
3	1	6	5	2	7	4	9	8
8	5	2	3	4	9	6	7	1

15

3	4	8	5	9	2	1	7	6
6	5	7	4	3	1	8	2	9
9	1	2	6	8	7	3	4	5
2	3	4	8	7	6	5	9	1
7	8	6	9	1	5	4	3	2
1	9	5	2	4	3	6	8	7
5	2	9	3	6	8	7	1	4
4	7	3	1	5	9	2	6	8
8	6	1	7	2	4	9	5	3

16

9	3	4	8	6	2	7	1	5
6	1	7	5	4	3	2	9	8
5	8	2	7	1	9	6	4	3
8	6	5	2	3	1	4	7	9
2	4	3	9	7	5	8	6	1
7	9	1	4	8	6	3	5	2
4	7	9	1	2	8	5	3	6
3	5	8	6	9	4	1	2	7
1	2	6	3	5	7	9	8	4

17

2	8	9	6	4	5	1	3	7
6	7	4	1	8	3	2	9	5
3	1	5	7	2	9	4	8	6
7	6	8	5	9	4	3	2	1
4	5	3	8	1	2	7	6	9
9	2	1	3	6	7	5	4	8
1	4	6	2	5	8	9	7	3
8	3	2	9	7	1	6	5	4
5	9	7	4	3	6	8	1	2

18

7	5	4	3	6	2	8	9	1
1	2	6	8	9	5	7	4	3
3	9	8	4	7	1	6	5	2
2	4	1	5	8	3	9	6	7
5	6	7	1	4	9	3	2	8
9	8	3	7	2	6	4	1	5
8	1	5	6	3	4	2	7	9
4	7	9	2	1	8	5	3	6
6	3	2	9	5	7	1	8	4

19

2	8	1	6	5	7	4	9	3
5	6	4	8	9	3	1	7	2
9	7	3	4	1	2	6	8	5
1	9	5	7	2	4	3	6	8
7	2	6	1	3	8	5	4	9
3	4	8	5	6	9	2	1	7
4	5	7	2	8	6	9	3	1
6	1	9	3	7	5	8	2	4
8	3	2	9	4	1	7	5	6

20

2	4	7	6	1	8	9	5	3
9	6	1	3	5	2	4	7	8
5	3	8	9	4	7	2	1	6
3	8	9	2	6	5	1	4	7
1	2	6	7	9	4	8	3	5
4	7	5	1	8	3	6	9	2
8	9	2	5	7	1	3	6	4
7	1	4	8	3	6	5	2	9
6	5	3	4	2	9	7	8	1

21

1	7	4	5	9	6	2	3	8
2	5	3	4	1	8	9	7	6
8	6	9	2	3	7	4	5	1
9	3	1	8	4	5	7	6	2
6	4	5	7	2	1	3	8	9
7	8	2	3	6	9	5	1	4
3	1	6	9	5	2	8	4	7
5	9	8	6	7	4	1	2	3
4	2	7	1	8	3	6	9	5

22

9	3	8	5	1	7	4	6	2
1	6	2	9	4	3	7	8	5
5	4	7	6	2	8	9	3	1
3	8	1	4	5	2	6	9	7
4	9	5	3	7	6	1	2	8
2	7	6	8	9	1	5	4	3
6	2	9	1	3	5	8	7	4
7	5	4	2	8	9	3	1	6
8	1	3	7	6	4	2	5	9

23

5	2	4	6	1	9	7	3	8
3	9	6	2	7	8	5	1	4
7	8	1	3	5	4	6	2	9
9	1	3	7	2	6	8	4	5
2	4	7	8	3	5	9	6	1
6	5	8	9	4	1	3	7	2
8	3	5	1	6	2	4	9	7
4	7	2	5	9	3	1	8	6
1	6	9	4	8	7	2	5	3

24

4	5	8	2	9	6	3	1	7
2	6	1	8	7	3	4	9	5
9	7	3	5	1	4	2	6	8
6	2	5	7	4	8	1	3	9
8	1	9	3	6	5	7	4	2
3	4	7	1	2	9	5	8	6
1	8	6	4	5	7	9	2	3
7	9	4	6	3	2	8	5	1
5	3	2	9	8	1	6	7	4

25

8	3	7	2	6	4	5	1	9
1	4	6	9	5	8	3	7	2
5	2	9	1	7	3	4	8	6
6	9	5	7	4	1	2	3	8
2	7	3	5	8	9	1	6	4
4	1	8	3	2	6	9	5	7
7	8	1	4	3	2	6	9	5
3	5	4	6	9	7	8	2	1
9	6	2	8	1	5	7	4	3

26

5	2	8	6	9	7	1	3	4
9	3	7	1	8	4	5	6	2
6	1	4	3	5	2	7	9	8
1	4	5	7	2	6	3	8	9
7	6	9	5	3	8	2	4	1
2	8	3	4	1	9	6	7	5
3	7	2	9	4	5	8	1	6
4	5	6	8	7	1	9	2	3
8	9	1	2	6	3	4	5	7

27

9	4	2	1	7	8	6	5	3
6	7	8	3	5	4	1	2	9
3	5	1	2	6	9	4	8	7
7	3	4	9	8	5	2	6	1
2	6	5	4	3	1	9	7	8
8	1	9	7	2	6	3	4	5
4	2	7	8	1	3	5	9	6
1	8	6	5	9	2	7	3	4
5	9	3	6	4	7	8	1	2

28

3	9	2	5	6	7	1	8	4
8	6	1	3	9	4	5	2	7
5	7	4	2	8	1	6	3	9
4	8	3	9	5	6	2	7	1
9	2	5	1	7	8	3	4	6
6	1	7	4	3	2	9	5	8
2	3	8	7	1	9	4	6	5
7	4	9	6	2	5	8	1	3
1	5	6	8	4	3	7	9	2

29

7	4	2	8	5	1	9	3	6
5	9	6	3	4	2	1	7	8
8	3	1	9	7	6	5	2	4
3	8	4	7	2	9	6	1	5
9	6	7	1	8	5	3	4	2
1	2	5	4	6	3	8	9	7
2	5	9	6	1	4	7	8	3
6	1	8	2	3	7	4	5	9
4	7	3	5	9	8	2	6	1

30

1	2	9	3	8	4	7	6	5
4	6	5	9	7	2	1	3	8
8	3	7	1	6	5	4	9	2
3	8	1	4	2	7	6	5	9
5	4	2	8	9	6	3	1	7
9	7	6	5	3	1	8	2	4
7	5	3	2	1	8	9	4	6
6	9	4	7	5	3	2	8	1
2	1	8	6	4	9	5	7	3

31

9	7	5	1	2	4	3	8	6
2	8	4	6	3	5	1	7	9
3	1	6	9	8	7	4	2	5
6	5	7	4	1	8	2	9	3
1	4	3	5	9	2	8	6	7
8	2	9	3	7	6	5	1	4
5	3	2	7	6	1	9	4	8
4	6	8	2	5	9	7	3	1
7	9	1	8	4	3	6	5	2

32

2	9	1	5	3	7	4	8	6
6	4	8	2	1	9	3	5	7
3	5	7	4	6	8	2	9	1
1	2	9	3	7	5	6	4	8
7	3	5	6	8	4	1	2	9
8	6	4	1	9	2	7	3	5
5	7	3	8	4	6	9	1	2
9	1	2	7	5	3	8	6	4
4	8	6	9	2	1	5	7	3

33

9	1	6	8	5	7	4	3	2
2	3	7	4	1	9	5	8	6
8	4	5	2	6	3	9	1	7
3	9	4	7	8	2	6	5	1
6	2	1	9	3	5	7	4	8
7	5	8	6	4	1	3	2	9
1	7	2	5	9	4	8	6	3
5	6	3	1	7	8	2	9	4
4	8	9	3	2	6	1	7	5

34

3	4	5	1	7	2	6	8	9
2	6	7	9	5	8	3	4	1
9	1	8	4	3	6	2	5	7
7	8	9	5	2	3	4	1	6
6	5	3	7	1	4	8	9	2
4	2	1	8	6	9	5	7	3
1	9	6	3	8	5	7	2	4
8	3	4	2	9	7	1	6	5
5	7	2	6	4	1	9	3	8

35

7	2	3	1	5	4	6	9	8
4	9	8	3	6	7	5	2	1
1	6	5	9	8	2	4	3	7
2	3	7	4	9	8	1	5	6
5	1	6	2	7	3	8	4	9
9	8	4	6	1	5	3	7	2
3	7	1	8	4	9	2	6	5
8	5	2	7	3	6	9	1	4
6	4	9	5	2	1	7	8	3

36

1	8	3	4	5	9	2	6	7
9	5	4	7	2	6	3	1	8
7	2	6	1	8	3	9	5	4
6	1	5	2	4	7	8	3	9
8	9	7	5	3	1	6	4	2
4	3	2	6	9	8	1	7	5
5	7	8	3	1	2	4	9	6
3	6	9	8	7	4	5	2	1
2	4	1	9	6	5	7	8	3

37

1	2	6	7	8	9	4	5	3
3	5	8	4	2	1	7	9	6
9	7	4	3	6	5	1	8	2
2	6	1	9	3	8	5	4	7
8	4	5	2	7	6	9	3	1
7	9	3	1	5	4	2	6	8
5	1	7	8	4	3	6	2	9
6	3	2	5	9	7	8	1	4
4	8	9	6	1	2	3	7	5

38

6	7	4	8	3	5	1	9	2
8	1	3	9	2	7	5	4	6
5	9	2	4	1	6	3	7	8
7	4	6	5	9	2	8	3	1
3	8	1	7	6	4	2	5	9
9	2	5	1	8	3	4	6	7
2	3	7	6	4	1	9	8	5
4	6	8	2	5	9	7	1	3
1	5	9	3	7	8	6	2	4

39

5	8	3	1	7	4	6	2	9
1	4	2	9	5	6	8	7	3
6	7	9	3	2	8	4	5	1
2	9	7	5	4	1	3	6	8
4	3	6	7	8	9	5	1	2
8	1	5	2	6	3	7	9	4
9	6	8	4	1	7	2	3	5
3	5	4	6	9	2	1	8	7
7	2	1	8	3	5	9	4	6

40

6	3	8	9	2	7	1	4	5
2	7	9	4	5	1	3	8	6
5	1	4	8	6	3	7	9	2
4	5	3	7	8	6	2	1	9
8	6	7	1	9	2	5	3	4
9	2	1	3	4	5	6	7	8
1	9	5	6	3	4	8	2	7
3	4	6	2	7	8	9	5	1
7	8	2	5	1	9	4	6	3

41

1	6	3	8	2	7	9	4	5
9	8	2	4	5	1	6	7	3
4	5	7	3	9	6	8	2	1
8	2	4	1	6	5	3	9	7
5	3	6	7	4	9	1	8	2
7	1	9	2	8	3	4	5	6
2	9	5	6	3	8	7	1	4
6	4	1	9	7	2	5	3	8
3	7	8	5	1	4	2	6	9

42

3	6	9	7	4	2	8	1	5
4	5	1	9	3	8	6	7	2
2	7	8	5	6	1	4	3	9
6	4	3	8	7	9	2	5	1
9	2	5	4	1	3	7	8	6
1	8	7	6	2	5	9	4	3
7	1	2	3	9	4	5	6	8
8	9	6	1	5	7	3	2	4
5	3	4	2	8	6	1	9	7

43

7	1	9	3	2	8	6	4	5
5	3	4	7	9	6	8	2	1
2	8	6	4	5	1	9	7	3
4	5	3	8	7	2	1	6	9
6	9	7	5	1	4	2	3	8
8	2	1	6	3	9	7	5	4
9	4	8	2	6	3	5	1	7
3	7	2	1	8	5	4	9	6
1	6	5	9	4	7	3	8	2

44

4	2	5	1	3	6	9	8	7
7	1	9	4	8	2	3	6	5
3	6	8	5	9	7	2	1	4
8	9	7	3	6	5	4	2	1
6	5	3	2	4	1	8	7	9
1	4	2	9	7	8	5	3	6
2	3	4	7	1	9	6	5	8
5	7	6	8	2	4	1	9	3
9	8	1	6	5	3	7	4	2

45

9	3	5	2	8	6	4	7	1
6	8	7	1	5	4	2	3	9
2	4	1	7	9	3	8	5	6
8	6	2	5	1	7	9	4	3
5	1	3	4	6	9	7	2	8
7	9	4	3	2	8	1	6	5
1	5	6	8	4	2	3	9	7
3	2	9	6	7	1	5	8	4
4	7	8	9	3	5	6	1	2

46

1	7	6	3	4	2	9	8	5
2	3	9	5	7	8	6	4	1
8	5	4	9	6	1	3	2	7
3	4	2	1	8	9	5	7	6
7	6	8	4	3	5	2	1	9
5	9	1	7	2	6	4	3	8
9	8	5	2	1	4	7	6	3
4	1	3	6	9	7	8	5	2
6	2	7	8	5	3	1	9	4

47

5	6	2	4	3	7	8	9	1
1	9	8	6	2	5	7	4	3
3	7	4	1	8	9	2	5	6
6	1	9	8	5	4	3	2	7
2	8	5	7	9	3	1	6	4
4	3	7	2	1	6	9	8	5
8	4	1	3	6	2	5	7	9
7	5	3	9	4	8	6	1	2
9	2	6	5	7	1	4	3	8

48

8	7	2	4	3	9	5	6	1
4	1	5	7	2	6	9	8	3
9	6	3	8	1	5	4	2	7
6	5	7	3	8	1	2	4	9
2	3	8	9	6	4	1	7	5
1	9	4	2	5	7	6	3	8
3	4	6	1	9	8	7	5	2
7	2	1	5	4	3	8	9	6
5	8	9	6	7	2	3	1	4

49

1	8	7	4	9	6	2	5	3
3	4	5	2	1	7	8	9	6
2	9	6	5	8	3	4	1	7
7	1	9	8	5	2	3	6	4
8	6	4	7	3	9	5	2	1
5	2	3	6	4	1	7	8	9
4	7	1	9	2	5	6	3	8
9	5	8	3	6	4	1	7	2
6	3	2	1	7	8	9	4	5

50

8	4	9	3	5	2	1	6	7
6	3	7	1	9	4	8	5	2
2	1	5	6	7	8	9	4	3
5	7	4	8	2	6	3	9	1
1	8	3	9	4	7	5	2	6
9	6	2	5	3	1	4	7	8
3	2	8	4	6	5	7	1	9
4	9	6	7	1	3	2	8	5
7	5	1	2	8	9	6	3	4

51

8	1	5	3	6	2	9	4	7
7	9	2	1	4	5	3	6	8
4	6	3	7	9	8	5	2	1
1	5	8	2	7	9	4	3	6
3	4	6	8	5	1	7	9	2
9	2	7	4	3	6	8	1	5
5	3	1	9	2	7	6	8	4
6	8	9	5	1	4	2	7	3
2	7	4	6	8	3	1	5	9

52

3	5	2	9	1	4	6	7	8
9	1	7	8	5	6	2	3	4
8	6	4	2	3	7	5	1	9
7	2	3	4	8	5	1	9	6
6	9	1	3	7	2	8	4	5
5	4	8	1	6	9	3	2	7
1	3	6	7	4	8	9	5	2
4	8	9	5	2	3	7	6	1
2	7	5	6	9	1	4	8	3

53

1	4	7	2	6	3	8	5	9
2	9	8	4	1	5	3	7	6
5	3	6	8	9	7	2	4	1
4	6	2	5	7	9	1	3	8
9	8	3	6	4	1	5	2	7
7	1	5	3	8	2	9	6	4
3	7	4	1	2	8	6	9	5
8	2	9	7	5	6	4	1	3
6	5	1	9	3	4	7	8	2

54

5	7	9	6	1	8	3	4	2
8	2	4	5	7	3	6	1	9
3	1	6	4	2	9	8	5	7
4	6	8	7	5	1	2	9	3
7	9	2	3	6	4	1	8	5
1	5	3	8	9	2	7	6	4
9	4	1	2	3	6	5	7	8
6	3	7	9	8	5	4	2	1
2	8	5	1	4	7	9	3	6

55

6	7	4	9	5	1	3	2	8
3	8	9	7	2	6	1	5	4
5	1	2	3	4	8	9	7	6
8	3	7	1	6	9	5	4	2
9	4	6	5	3	2	8	1	7
2	5	1	8	7	4	6	3	9
4	9	8	2	1	5	7	6	3
1	6	3	4	9	7	2	8	5
7	2	5	6	8	3	4	9	1

56

1	3	4	5	7	8	9	6	2
8	9	5	2	6	4	1	3	7
7	6	2	3	9	1	8	5	4
5	2	8	7	3	6	4	1	9
4	7	9	8	1	5	3	2	6
6	1	3	9	4	2	7	8	5
9	5	1	6	8	7	2	4	3
2	8	7	4	5	3	6	9	1
3	4	6	1	2	9	5	7	8

57

2	8	9	6	7	4	3	1	5
4	7	6	5	1	3	8	9	2
5	3	1	9	8	2	4	7	6
3	1	5	2	9	8	7	6	4
8	9	2	4	6	7	1	5	3
7	6	4	3	5	1	9	2	8
6	4	7	1	3	5	2	8	9
1	5	3	8	2	9	6	4	7
9	2	8	7	4	6	5	3	1

58

4	8	7	9	5	3	6	2	1
1	6	3	4	2	7	5	8	9
5	2	9	6	1	8	7	4	3
7	3	2	5	9	1	8	6	4
9	4	5	8	6	2	1	3	7
8	1	6	7	3	4	2	9	5
2	5	8	3	7	9	4	1	6
6	9	4	1	8	5	3	7	2
3	7	1	2	4	6	9	5	8

59

7	2	5	8	3	4	1	9	6
6	3	9	2	1	7	8	5	4
1	8	4	5	6	9	2	3	7
2	6	7	9	5	1	3	4	8
3	5	1	4	2	8	7	6	9
9	4	8	6	7	3	5	1	2
8	9	3	7	4	5	6	2	1
4	1	2	3	8	6	9	7	5
5	7	6	1	9	2	4	8	3

60

5	4	6	8	1	3	2	9	7
1	3	7	2	9	6	5	4	8
2	8	9	7	5	4	6	1	3
7	6	1	9	4	2	3	8	5
4	5	2	3	6	8	1	7	9
3	9	8	1	7	5	4	2	6
9	2	4	5	3	7	8	6	1
6	7	3	4	8	1	9	5	2
8	1	5	6	2	9	7	3	4

61

8	4	9	7	3	6	2	1	5
6	7	5	1	4	2	3	8	9
1	3	2	5	9	8	7	6	4
2	6	8	3	7	4	9	5	1
3	9	1	8	2	5	6	4	7
7	5	4	9	6	1	8	3	2
4	2	3	6	1	9	5	7	8
5	1	6	2	8	7	4	9	3
9	8	7	4	5	3	1	2	6

62

7	4	5	9	2	1	8	6	3
2	9	3	8	4	6	1	5	7
8	6	1	3	5	7	2	4	9
5	8	6	7	3	2	9	1	4
4	2	9	1	6	8	7	3	5
1	3	7	5	9	4	6	2	8
6	7	8	4	1	3	5	9	2
3	5	2	6	7	9	4	8	1
9	1	4	2	8	5	3	7	6

63

3	8	6	9	4	5	7	1	2
9	2	1	7	8	6	3	4	5
4	7	5	2	1	3	8	6	9
7	3	2	8	9	4	6	5	1
5	9	4	6	3	1	2	7	8
6	1	8	5	7	2	9	3	4
2	4	7	3	5	8	1	9	6
1	6	3	4	2	9	5	8	7
8	5	9	1	6	7	4	2	3

64

3	5	6	4	1	2	9	8	7
1	2	7	9	5	8	4	3	6
9	8	4	7	6	3	5	2	1
4	7	1	5	2	9	3	6	8
5	6	3	8	4	7	1	9	2
8	9	2	6	3	1	7	5	4
7	1	8	2	9	5	6	4	3
2	4	9	3	7	6	8	1	5
6	3	5	1	8	4	2	7	9

65

1	9	8	4	6	7	3	5	2
4	7	6	2	5	3	9	8	1
3	2	5	9	8	1	4	6	7
7	8	3	6	4	5	2	1	9
9	5	4	7	1	2	6	3	8
6	1	2	8	3	9	5	7	4
2	3	9	1	7	6	8	4	5
8	6	1	5	2	4	7	9	3
5	4	7	3	9	8	1	2	6

66

5	2	9	1	7	8	6	3	4
3	8	7	2	4	6	9	1	5
1	4	6	9	5	3	8	2	7
2	9	1	8	3	4	7	5	6
6	7	8	5	2	1	4	9	3
4	3	5	7	6	9	1	8	2
8	6	2	4	9	5	3	7	1
7	1	4	3	8	2	5	6	9
9	5	3	6	1	7	2	4	8

67

8	3	4	7	6	9	5	2	1
9	5	1	4	8	2	6	3	7
7	2	6	3	5	1	8	4	9
3	6	2	9	1	5	4	7	8
1	4	9	8	7	6	2	5	3
5	7	8	2	4	3	1	9	6
4	9	7	1	2	8	3	6	5
6	8	3	5	9	4	7	1	2
2	1	5	6	3	7	9	8	4

68

2	9	7	8	6	3	4	5	1
6	5	3	1	4	2	8	9	7
8	1	4	9	7	5	2	6	3
1	6	2	7	3	9	5	4	8
4	7	8	2	5	6	3	1	9
9	3	5	4	8	1	6	7	2
7	2	6	3	1	4	9	8	5
3	4	1	5	9	8	7	2	6
5	8	9	6	2	7	1	3	4

69

8	3	5	6	2	1	4	9	7
9	6	4	8	3	7	5	1	2
2	1	7	5	4	9	3	6	8
7	5	6	4	8	2	1	3	9
1	8	3	9	5	6	2	7	4
4	9	2	7	1	3	8	5	6
6	4	8	3	9	5	7	2	1
3	7	1	2	6	8	9	4	5
5	2	9	1	7	4	6	8	3

70

8	1	4	3	7	6	9	2	5
5	7	6	2	9	8	3	1	4
9	3	2	1	4	5	8	7	6
1	4	9	8	6	3	2	5	7
6	8	5	7	2	1	4	9	3
7	2	3	4	5	9	1	6	8
3	6	8	9	1	7	5	4	2
4	9	7	5	8	2	6	3	1
2	5	1	6	3	4	7	8	9

71

4	6	8	2	7	9	1	5	3
1	7	2	3	5	4	8	6	9
9	5	3	1	6	8	4	7	2
5	1	6	4	3	2	7	9	8
3	8	4	9	1	7	5	2	6
7	2	9	6	8	5	3	1	4
6	4	7	8	9	1	2	3	5
2	3	1	5	4	6	9	8	7
8	9	5	7	2	3	6	4	1

72

6	1	9	8	7	5	3	4	2
8	5	2	3	6	4	1	7	9
4	3	7	1	9	2	5	6	8
1	6	8	5	3	9	4	2	7
3	7	4	2	8	1	6	9	5
9	2	5	7	4	6	8	3	1
2	4	1	9	5	3	7	8	6
5	8	3	6	2	7	9	1	4
7	9	6	4	1	8	2	5	3

73

8	7	1	4	2	5	3	6	9
6	9	2	3	7	1	5	8	4
5	4	3	8	6	9	1	7	2
3	2	8	1	5	4	6	9	7
9	1	6	2	3	7	4	5	8
7	5	4	6	9	8	2	1	3
1	8	9	5	4	2	7	3	6
2	6	7	9	1	3	8	4	5
4	3	5	7	8	6	9	2	1